I was the hospice nurse who participated in the coming to rest described in this book. It was a beautiful and useful closure for a whole community. Since then as the Director of Nursing of a home care agency I have introduced others to this compassionate and healing way of taking charge of the body of a loved one.

Frances Woollard, Director of Nursing,
Kohala Home Health, Big Island, Hawaii.

Our family did a lot of what this book encourages us to do. It is so refreshing to see something in print that will help others help their loved ones. HURRAH for the authors' sensitive yet thorough and precise steps in helping us to do it ourselves.

Lani Bowman,
Kohala, Big Island, Hawaii.

This book is published by Dovetail, Inc.

All rights reserved

dovetail@funeralresources.com

(808)773-9580

Printed in the United States of America.

Copyright © 1998 by Julie Wiskind and Richard Spiegal

ISBN 0-9657593-6-9

Library of Congress Catalogue Card Number 97-092227

Cover design / photo Joseph Dea
Spiral graphic moses / hawaii

Credit Card Orders   (800)431-1579
Fax Orders   (914)835-0398

Mail Orders   Dovetail
                          P.O. Box 1720
                          Kamuela, HI 96743

One copy $14.00
Two copies $19.20
Eight copies $57.60
First class postage paid
Add $2.00 for each additional address
There is an order form in the back of this book.

COMING TO REST

A Guide to
Caring for Our Own Dead

by
Julie Wiskind
and Richard Spiegel

P   R   E   F   A   C   E

You don't have to call the funeral director when someone in your family dies. Following state Health Department guidelines, you and your family can remain with the body and bring it to the crematory or cemetery yourselves, in your own car or van.

Making the funeral arrangements can be as simple as filling out some forms and taking care of the transportation. It will save you money, but the value to you may be deeper and more far-reaching than the money savings. You will be able to finish the care of someone you love in a way that reflects your own traditions and sense of dignity. The funeral can be simple and matter of fact. It can also be the basis for an intimate and powerful occasion.

This book will tell you what you need to know to provide a safe and legal funeral for one of your own. Although we have tried to make certain that all the information we present here is accurate and complete. We cannot assume responsibility for any adverse effects resulting from using this information, nor from our inadvertent oversight of information that might be relevant.

Regulations in the following states prohibit or seriously restrict families from acting as their own funeral director: Connecticut, Illinois, Indiana, Louisiana, Michigan, Nebraska, New Hampshire, New Jersey and New York.

While we encourage you to consider this alternative to a commercial funeral, neither the authors nor those at Dovetail are licensed to provide, nor do we provide, legal advice or professional funeral services.

By writing this book, it has not been our purpose to disparage any group, practice, or institution. If this has happened it has been without our intention and we sincerely apologize for it.

We are very interested in hearing your thoughts and experiences. Please let us know what choices you have made, what difficulties you have encountered, and what blessings you may have received from a private family funeral. Your comments will help us with future editions of this book.

If you would like your local hospice or home care agency to have information about non-commercial funerals, please let us know. We will make sure that they do.

Thank you.

Dovetail, Resources for a Family Funeral

This book grew from the response of a particular community on the Big Island of Hawaii to the loss of a cherished friend, Laura Spiegel. Without the courage and love of the community for her, for one another, and for this project, the book would not have been written. We thank especially Frances Woollard and Mac McCurdy for their good will and support. So many others have helped with encouragement and expertise. We are deeply grateful to Patricia Anderson, Margaret and David Balamuthe, Dwayne Banks, Bonnie Beardsley, Ruthie and Jim Bernaert, Diana Blackford, Nancy Bouvet, Eric Brown, Gianni and Vikki Catellacci, Margaret Chester, Dennis Cigainero, Craig Clyde, Randolf Croft, Bryce Fillmore, Elizabeth Frankin, Peter Frost, Cate Gable, Rondi Gilbert, Michael and Rocket Glass, Carolyn Gordon, Judy Graham, Virginia Hammon, Greatha, Walter, Jacob and Christopher Jaeckle, Denise and Eric Johnsen, Bart and Corey Jones, Rosemary Jones, Nora Knowles, Fred Kraft, Colleenah Lawrence, Karen Leonard, Ben Lawrence, Theresa Y. Lee, Johnnie Luane, Stephanie Mallard, Shelley Massman, Jane Mauldon, Lucy Mauldon, Evelyn McCarthy, Sara McCay, Leroy Montana, moses/ hawaii, Gordon and Laura Motta, Rion Noone, Tom Noone, Stephen Oldfather, Osa Paglinawon, Matt Pearce, Helga Prosak, Dean and Anne Prosser, Jim Quinton, John Renfroe, Gayle Robinson, David Rose, Flo Rosiello, Carol Salisbury, Ellen and Bob Seltzer, Shakti, Laurene Share, Suzanne Simonds, Shaina Spiegel, Don Spinell, Betsy Tabac, Kristin and Stbon Tarnas, Bob Vogelsang, Linda Waldron, Tom and Brenda Walker, Richard Waller, Beverly Warns, Kiana Waters, Jay West, John White, Jan and Sam Whitehead, Judy Whiteside, Rick and Kristie Willits, Becky Winters, Gabriel Wiskind, Adam Wiskind, and Vicki Woollard.

When the Sabbath was over, Mary Magdalene, Mary the mother of James, and Salome, bought spices so that they might go to anoint Jesus' body.

MARK 16

Members of the Chevra (the self-help burial society), when asked why they "subject" themselves to this task, respond that for them this is the highest mitzva (blessing). One member stated succinctly, "The met (body), like an infant, has to be taken care of. We try to handle him gently, in a caressing and comforting manner. He can do nothing for himself; we must do for him. I hope when my time comes, someone will do the same for me."

A Plain Pine Box – A Return to Simple Jewish Funerals and
Eternal Traditions by Rabbi Arnold M. Goodman
KTAV Publishing House

C O N T E N T S

PREFACE 4

MAKING THE BED (A POEM) 12

COMING TO REST 13

OUR AMERICAN FUNERALS 17

CHANGING APPROACHES TO DEATH ... 19

WHEN YOU NEED THE
FUNERAL DIRECTOR 23

THE FAMILY FUNERAL 26

   HOME AND FAMILY 28

   ALONGSIDE ME (A POEM) 30

   GRIEF 31

   TAKING CARE OF THE BODY 32

     Washing or Purifying the Body 32

     Laying Out the Body 33

     Timing 34

     Health and Safety 36

     The Casket 37
       Buying a Casket 37
       Plans for a Simple Homemade Casket 38

   TRANSPORTATION 42

   CEREMONY 43

THE LEGAL REQUIREMENTS 45

WHO CAN TAKE RESPONSIBILITY 46
Family, Friends, and Religious Groups .. 46
Funeral Director Required 48

HOW IT WORKS 49

PAPERWORK 52
The Death Certificate 52
The Disposition - Transit Permit 54
The Cremation Permit 55

TIMING FOR THE PAPERWORK 56

THE MEDICAL EXAMINER 57
Autopsy 57
Contagious Diseases 57

BURIAL OR CREMATION 58

FINDING A CEMETERY OR CREMATORY .. 60

BURIAL 62
Choices at the Cemetery 62
Paying for the Burial 64

CREMATION 67

BODY AND ORGAN DONATION 69

A P P E N D I X E S

FUNERAL PLANNING GUIDE.................. 72

CHECKLIST FOR
THE DAY OF THE FUNERAL 76

THE DEATH CERTIFICATE 79

THE OBITUARY NOTICE 83

COMMERCIAL FUNERAL OPTIONS 84

CHART OF STATE FUNERAL
REGULATIONS 86

WHERE TO GET MORE HELP 96

LETTING GO SLOWLY (A POEM) 100

MAKING THE BED

Richard Spiegel

Making the bed
your side
unslept in
now
for more than a year.

Still
I pat your pillows
smooth the quilt you made

moving my hands
through the emptiness
on your side
of the bed.

COMING TO REST

When death came to our wonderful friend and wife, Laura, in February of 1993, we found, without really meaning to, that it was possible to file the simple paperwork and to bring her body to the crematory privately, in our own time, in our own car, after our own good-byes and prayers. There were no legal or health reasons for us to hire a professional as an intermediary for this deeply felt occasion.

For her last months of life Laura had made it clear that she would like to be at home, not in a hospital. While she was home, her friends and family became a daily part of her struggle for strength and clarity as her body declined from cancer. With the help of hospice, we took care of her physical needs and she allowed us to share her most intimate experience, the death of her body.

After personally caring for her and sharing the intimacy of her death, it felt inappropriate and unnecessary to hire someone to take Laura's body away. In one sense the hard part was over. All that was needed now was for us to bring the body to where it would come to rest. For our own benefit, for the completion it would allow us, we wanted to continue this final part of her care in the personal, hands-on way we had been doing. It was a way for us to bring closure to what had been the focus of our lives for the past weeks and months, and a way for us to honor someone we loved.

One phone call led to the amazing discovery of just how simple making the funeral could be. We learned that, after we filed the death certificate at the Department of Health, we could notify the crematory and bring the body to them in our own car.

That day was a remarkable day for all of us. None of us had been part of anything like it before. Responding to our own needs and to the needs of the situation, the day unfolded naturally, without advanced planning.

Fran, the hospice nurse, came to pronounce death and to offer moral support. We began to call close friends and family. Some of them came to the house with their children and many came with food. We answered the phone and straightened the house and talked and cried together. A police officer came and sheepishly asked a few questions. There was time for solitary walks and meditation. We looked at old photos and at Laura's fondest possessions, and we described the events leading up to her death to those who just arrived.

A friend called the crematory to schedule a time for our arrival. Another friend built a beautiful wood pallet. He also brought the station wagon we would use to bring her body to the crematory. It was good to be together and to have something useful to do.

Some of us chose to spend time and to say our personal good-byes and prayers at Laura's bedside. Others did not. In our own time and in the informal, familiar surroundings of Laura's home, the shocking and abrupt reality of her death was brought home to our everyday lives.

The doctor came with the death certificate and Richard, Laura's husband, filled out the family history section of the form. When it was completed it was brought to the Health Department office in town.

For some of Laura's friends it was natural to prepare her body since we had been caring for her at home for weeks. Her face had relaxed into a peaceful expression. Far from being repelled, washing her body awakened a tenderness in us that we had rarely experienced before. We wrapped her body in a clean white sheet and her favorite shawl, gathered Hawaiian ti leaves and flowers for the pallet and laid her gently on it.

When all was ready, a few of us, including Richard, their two daughters, Kristin and Shaina, and Kristin's husband Stbon, carried the body to the station wagon and drove in a small procession to the crematory. The crematory staff waited while we carried the body one last time.

This funeral, which cost $300, enabled us to respond privately and informally to our own need to say good-bye. We began our grief together, each of us feeling the simple, direct, hands-on support of friends and family.

There would be a formal memorial service for the larger community in a few days time. But, the funeral itself, without any planning, was a powerful occasion, useful to us emotionally and spiritually. Perhaps because it was a private occasion, personal and familiar, we could begin to sense the balance between activity and quiet, friendship and solitude, that we would need to find peace, eventually, with Laura's death.

 # OUR AMERICAN FUNERALS

Not so long ago in this country, most families carried their own loved ones to the cemetery for burial.

When someone died the family made a casket themselves or ordered one from a local carpenter. The body remained in the parlor for a day or so until the family assembled and the casket was delivered. When it was time, they gathered for a procession to the graveyard, followed by a simple burial ceremony.

Most Americans replaced this family funeral tradition with a commercial funeral after the Civil War, which introduced the practice of embalming. During the Civil War, before refrigeration was available, embalming was used to preserve the bodies of soldiers for the trip back to a distant home for burial. It was embalming which allowed Abraham Lincoln's funeral train to tour the country before he was buried. Almost uniquely in the world Americans of the time adopted embalming as a preferred funeral practice.

After the Civil War embalming became popular among civilians, and embalmers began to call themselves "morticians". Morticians provided "parlors" to newly urbanized Americans who didn't have space at home for a large gathering, and carriages to those without their own means of transportation.

They helped the family fill out the death certificate. They provided caskets for purchase. They scheduled arrivals at the cemetery and thus became "funeral directors".

The early funeral parlor was a small family business, often associated with a particular community or ethnic group. The director's family would live on the premises, usually in a large house. Often they were respected leaders in the community. The funeral director was well paid for a service which few were willing to do and which took some personal courage.

Today these small, community based, "mom and pop" funeral homes are disappearing fast. Their names, familiar to local residents, are retained by the multinational corporations which have bought them and now dominate the funeral industry. The three largest funeral companies bury one in four Americans who die. The largest of these companies, Service Corporation International is an extraordinarily profitable organization. It has sales totaling billions of dollars. It owns three thousand funeral homes, hundreds of cemeteries and crematories, and it is, currently buying funeral homes in Britain, France, Australia and elsewhere.

CHANGING APPROACHES TO DEATH

With the development of modern medicine and medical insurance in the twentieth century, Americans increasingly died in hospitals instead of at home. The commercial funeral industry flourished in this situation because once people were in the hands of professionals in an institution, it felt simpler and even appropriate for funeral professionals to remain in charge. Hospitals came to rely on funeral directors to remove bodies promptly and to lead the grieving family elsewhere.

Our society's boundless faith in modern medicine reflected a "never say die" attitude that was captured in the 1979 book *Celebrations of Death: The Anthropology of Mortuary Ritual* by Richard Huntington and Peter Metcalf (Cambridge University Press). In it Huntington and Metcalf describe our understandable, but overreaching attempt to prevail over a most awesome, heartbreaking aspect of our lives.

> "The majority of deaths now occur in hospitals where the fiction of probable recovery is often maintained until the person is near the point of death. The corpse is then promptly removed without the aid of the bereaved, who see it again only under very special circumstances, after it has been primped up to appear as if asleep."

We devoted great wealth and ingenuity to the task of denying a place for death in our busy lives, hoping that if we bought the services of competent medical and funeral professionals, while death might not disappear, it could perhaps be handled without painful personal involvement.

Soon the cost of this strategy became apparent. First, there were the enormous financial costs of a high-technology, professionally orchestrated death, from the hospital to the funeral home. Second, those spending the last part of their lives in an institution found themselves out of touch with the personal, traditional, and spiritual context of their ordinary lives.

The high cost and sense of alienation that often accompanied death in an institution, moved many Americans to seek a less expensive, more honest encounter with death. Privately and publicly, during the past 20 years, we have focused our attention on how we die. We seem determined not only to cut costs but also to make choices that allow death to deepen our life experience and humanize our institutions.

Religions have always tried to provide emotional comfort and spiritual perspective to their adherents at the time of death. But in the 1970s and 1980s Elizabeth Kubler-Ross, a physician, challenged us to acknowledge our fears and to talk with one another about our experiences with death and grief.

Popular books and magazines now explore aspects of death that formerly were taboo. The physical process of dying, care of the dying, patient control of the end of life decisions, suicide, grief, and life after death, are subjects of great interest and open discussion.

The Project On Death In America encourages people in government, the arts, and in educational and medical establishments to find ways to provide a responsive and compassionate institutional climate surrounding death and bereavement.

The Natural Death Center was formed to improve the quality of our deaths by fostering simple and green alternatives. They encourage non-commercial funerals, the integration of wildlife preserves with cemeteries and the use of death midwives, trained to help the dying through the time of transition.

Hospice and home health agencies now help families to provide a comfortable, peaceful place for dying at home. Their focus is not on curing but on keeping people pain-free while preserving the personal control and awareness that has made their lives worthwhile. The whole family is supported and put at ease by a staff that knows what to expect and how to proceed calmly as death arrives.

There are now people who are specifically trained to help the dying and their caregivers to use imminent death as background for learning forgiveness, acceptance, and grace. These facilitators see a chance at the time of physical separation, to heal what might have separated us for so long from ourselves and from one another. For them death becomes a path for a transformation of heart.

If you are interested in learning more about these ideas and groups, see the books and organizations listed in "Where to Get More Help" in the appendix.

WHEN YOU NEED THE FUNERAL DIRECTOR

Whoever is taking responsibility for the funeral, whether family member or professional funeral director, files the signed death certificate with the local office of the state Department of Health. The Department of Health registrar will then give them a permit to bring the covered body to the cemetery or crematory.

This seems simple enough, but before you decide that a non-commercial funeral is for your family, it is good to consider certain other important issues.

Comfort Level: Although the legal and physical requirements of the funeral are straightforward, many people simply will not feel comfortable unless there is a professional to handle the arrangements. This is an important time to respect your intuition. Stay within your level of comfort.

Support: It takes at least four people to share the emotional and physical burdens of the funeral. Four are needed to carry the casket. You must feel the support of one another at this time. If you are at odds with one another about whether a family funeral is appropriate, it probably is not a good idea to have one.

Responsibility: The death certificate must be signed by the physician who certifies the cause of death and by the family member or friend who accepts legal responsibility for carrying out Department of Health regulations. Although this responsibility can be freely taken by a family member or friend, only someone licensed by the state to provide funeral services can be paid to assume this responsibility.

State of Residence: The following states usually require that a professional funeral director participate, at one level or another, in each funeral: Connecticut, Illinois, Indiana, Louisiana, Michigan, Nebraska, New Hampshire, New Jersey, and New York. See the chapter "Who Can Take Legal Responsibility", for more details.

Transportation: A professional funeral director must be hired when the body is to be moved by public transportation such as by train or airplane. If the body is to be moved by private car out of state, contact the health authorities in the states you will pass through. They may require you to hire a professional.

Contagious Diseases: When the death is a result of a highly contagious disease, so designated by the Department of Health, a professional funeral director may be required. States differ in what they consider to be highly contagious. Only a few consider AIDS, hepatitis, and tuberculosis to be highly contagious in this context.

Embalming: In the United States, only a professional embalmer, working in a licensed funeral home, can embalm the body.

For thousands of years, people of different cultures embalmed the bodies of their loved ones after death. This practice was usually motivated by the religious belief that the soul, released from the body at death, could return later to reclaim the preserved body.

Embalming, as practiced by the modern funeral industry, is not a religious ritual. It is not practiced for public health reasons either, or for the long-term preservation of the body. Embalming is usually used to serve those who want the body of the deceased restored and suitable for open casket viewing a few days after death.

Embalming is rarely legally required. It is simply one of the options a funeral director offers. If you want this service you must hire a funeral director.

Embalming is one of a number of services offered by a modern funeral home that is beyond what is minimally necessary for the funeral. Some of the other options offered by the funeral home are discussed in "Commercial Funeral Options" in the appendix.

THE FAMILY FUNERAL

HOME AND FAMILY

ALONGSIDE ME (A POEM)

GRIEF

TAKING CARE OF THE BODY

Washing or Purifying the Body

Laying Out the Body

Timing

Health and Safety

The Casket
>Buying a Casket
>Plans for a Simple Homemade Casket

TRANSPORTATION

CEREMONY

THE FAMILY FUNERAL

This chapter presents an overview of family concerns at the time of the funeral. Although it includes information on grief and the funeral ceremony, the focus is on the practicalities of bringing the body from the place of death to the cemetery or the crematory in a safe, legal and dignified way.

As you read you will notice not only how simple arranging the funeral can be, but that much of what needs to be done can be anticipated and taken care of ahead of time. Although it is not absolutely necessary to plan ahead, if you have a chance to plan you will be able to talk with the appropriate agencies and avoid bureaucratic delays. There is a "Funeral Planning Guide" in the appendix of this book to help you organize your particular plans.

Some families make no funeral plans at all. Even without them, in most situations, as long as you are clear in your intention to provide the funeral yourselves, you should be able to proceed without difficulty. There is a "Checklist for the Day of the Funeral" in the appendix which you can use whether you have made any advanced plans or not.

HOME AND FAMILY

When a family member is near death there is an air of expectancy. The frequency of telephone calls increases among households. You prepare yourself for a change in your schedule and a tear in the fabric of the family. You may be aware that this event will refocus your life.

Although this may be a time of confusion, anger, and sadness, this can also be a time of acceptance. Perhaps you will take the opportunity to say good-bye, to express your love for one another, your forgiveness, and your gratitude.

As death approaches it is a good idea to locate the documents and information that you will need in the coming days. Put this guidebook in an easily accessible place together with:

- the will and the name, address, and phone number of the executor of the estate.
- any safety deposit box numbers and keys.
- the attorney's name, address, and phone number.
- any checking, saving, brokerage accounts, insurance policies, credit cards, and other assets.
- a blank book, so that when mourners arrive there is a place in which they can express their sentiments.
- a list by the telephone so that you can remember the messages left by callers.

Once it is clear that death has occurred take whatever time you need to become calm. Gather those closest.

Remember, this is not an emergency.

Phone the physician or home health nurse then phone friends and family.

ALONGSIDE ME

Richard Spiegel

An emptiness
moves alongside me
wherever I go
like a wake in the air
as I move
but not behind me
a space alongside me
The space you once filled.

It has impenetrable
bubble-like walls
I can gaze in
but I can't enter it
Yet it is attached to me
and stays with me.

It is what is left of you
outside of memory
It is the essence of you
still left behind
empty
yet palpable
a nothingness
of real proportion.

GRIEF

The time of the death is not always a time of strong and painful emotion. Often death is a relief for the survivors and a release for the deceased. Sometimes, however, when someone you love dies, the heart is laid open in grief. You are then vulnerable to waves of sadness, confusion, numbness, and anger which may hold you for many months or years.

You may find yourself in the initial shock of grief, when you can't bear to look at anybody or to join in the busyness of life. When this happens it is helpful if you remember to care for yourself – eat and drink water, shower, talk to someone, go out at night, look at the horizon (not just toward it), and keep moving your body (outside if possible). Most important, have patience. Grief has its own schedule.

In order to feel whole again you may also find it helpful to talk to others about your experience. Most people have had some experience with death, and some have come away from it kinder and wiser. Seek out these people. Choose someone who feels comfortable to you: a friend, a counselor, or perhaps a support group for those who have recently experienced a death.

There is a list of other helpful resources in the appendix. This is only a place to start. There are many books for the spirit and books for the emotions written by survivors for survivors.

TAKING CARE OF THE BODY

When death takes place in a hospital or nursing home, as most do, you can proceed with the funeral in a number of ways. If you like, once the paperwork is complete, you can personally transport the body to the cemetery or crematory without formalities.

If you need more time to prepare than the institution will allow you, or if you want a more private setting for your preparations, bring the body home first before proceeding to the crematory or the cemetery.

If you prefer, you can retain legal responsibility for the funeral, but not be involved with hands-on personal care of the body. Hire a mortuary transportation service or even an ambulance to bring the body from the hospital or nursing home to the crematory or the cemetery.

Washing or Purifying the Body

People in many cultures wash or purify the body before they dress it, or wrap it in a shroud, and place it in the casket. If you decide to do this, gather together grooming articles such as soaps, aromatic oils, brushes, and towels. The teeth can be cleaned, but do not remove any dentures, because you may not get them back in place.

Some people pour water over the body in ritual fashion, for purification. Many give the body a sponge bath. When you wash the body, it is important to complete the process before rigor mortis sets in. About two hours after death rigor mortis will stiffen the body and make it impossible to change its position. If this has been allowed to happen, it is best not to fight it. Understand that it is a temporary state. The stiffness will begin to dissipate four hours or so after it has fully set in.

In the days prior to the death, the appetite is often lost so kidney and bowel function may have shut down naturally. To be certain there is no leaking, particularly when moving the body, use a diaper, or place cotton in the rectum and the vagina, and a plastic bag or a condom over the penis. As further protection you may want to put plastic sheeting in the bottom of the casket.

You can disinfect soiled sheets and equipment with household bleach.

Laying Out the Body

Many cultures share the tradition of laying out the dead. As soon as possible remove any pillows from under the head and legs and lay the body flat in a peaceful pose. Close the eyes and the mouth. The eyes can be taped closed or weighted closed with a coin. The mouth will remain closed if a small, tightly-rolled cloth is placed firmly under the chin, or if the jaw is tied closed with a cloth soon after death.

You can use a shawl or sheet for a shroud, or the body can be dressed in formal or favorite clothing. Sometimes clothing is cut in the back to make dressing easier. You will want to keep the body as cool as possible so do not cover it with blankets.

A simple way to carry the body a short distance is to lift it by gripping the edges of a sheet underneath. Gripping the sheet also makes it easier to negotiate awkward turns in the house before you place the body in the casket.

Timing

The funeral must take place soon after the death. Though the rate the body decomposes varies with the temperature, it is not as swift and repelling as one might imagine. Leave an air conditioner on, make a mattress of dry ice, or use block ice near the body to keep the air cool, and if need be, wash the body again. The Massachusetts Department of Health states in a letter to local health officials in August 1996, that "the human body can be kept in a cool room for at least 24 hours before decomposition even begins to be a factor".

A few states specify precisely how much time can elapse between the death, and the burial or cremation. They usually allow twenty-four or forty-eight hours. California has a twenty-four hour rule that applies to funeral directors only, and not to independent families. This reveals the intention of the regulation, which is not to guard against health hazards from an unburied body, but to assure that the funeral director acts professionally by providing services promptly.

There are different religious beliefs about the timing of the funeral. In some traditions, the burial must take place as soon as possible, within twenty-four hours of the death. Other traditions insist that there be a waiting period of a few days before the body is moved at all.

Religious considerations are not the only reasons for delay of the funeral. Families may want to postpone the ceremony until distant relatives arrive, or there may still be questions about the cause of death. In addition, before cremation can take place in certain states, a precautionary waiting period of a day or two is required. See the "Chart of State Funeral Regulations" in the appendix for a list of the states in which a waiting period is required before cremation.

If disposition of the body is going to be delayed for more than a few days for any reason, refrigeration will probably be necessary. The morgue at a local hospital, crematory, or funeral home will, hopefully, be able to provide space when you need it.

Health and Safety

While individuals who do not have any infections prior to death present little or no infection risk after death, thorough hand washing after handling the body is always a good precaution.

For the family of those with infectious diseases such as AIDS, tuberculosis, or hepatitis, it is just as important to avoid contact with body fluids after death as it was before death because the live virus or bacterium does persist after death. However, the risk is no greater than before death. You can use latex gloves to avoid contact with any body fluids.

If you are unsure about making the funeral arrangements because of these diseases, you may want to check with your own physician or a public health official.

In most states the existence of AIDS, tuberculosis or hepatitis does not require special notification of the Medical Examiner or the involvement of a professional funeral director. When the death certificate indicates a highly contagious disease, you will be informed by the Department of Health.

The Casket

Buying a Casket

Commercial funeral directors use the word "casket" only when they speak of their high-end products of hardwood, steel or fiberglass that are lined with mattresses and pillows. These can easily cost thousands of dollars. Anything other than this is referred to by them as an "alternative container" or a "box". We will not make that distinction here.

A "casket", whether extremely expensive or simple and functional, is a safe and dignified way to carry the body. However, a casket is not required when cremation is chosen. You may be able to use a pallet or a stretcher. What is important is that you cover the body while in transit, that you carry the body in a careful and dignified manner, and that you respect public sensibilities.

By law, funeral homes must offer an alternative to their high-end casket. This "alternative container", usually fiberboard covered with felt, sells at the funeral home for $500-$1,000.

A "cremation box" is made of light-weight corrugated cardboard. It is sold by the crematory or by the funeral home for $15-$75. The cremation box is not designed to be hand carried, but to be placed on a gurney and rolled, so it will not have handles or a supported base. If the family decides to use a cremation box to carry the body, the cardboard base can be reinforced with plywood. It can then be hoisted on the shoulders for carrying.

You can order a casket from a local carpenter, or buy one at discount on the internet. These can be delivered overnight. In Europe and, increasingly, in the United States, caskets can be bought at a retail specialty store.

Plans for a Simple Homemade Casket

By law, families can provide their own casket, homemade or commercially produced, without being charged extra. Be sure that whatever you make is well fastened together with a rigid base. Don't make it too large. Twenty-five inches wide by fourteen inches high is a large size casket. Adjust the length to six or twelve inches longer than the body.

Someone with a few tools and a few skills can make the following strong and simple casket in three hours or so. We present a cutting diagram for both a large and a medium size casket. The sides are high enough in the large size for the bottom to be lined with a thin mattress. A similar design for a medium size casket is shallower. The end pieces either can be cut to the same height as the sides or a few inches longer to form legs. The legs add visual interest to this very simple box.

To make these caskets you will need:

Plywood: Two 3/4 inch sheets for a large size; one 3/4 inch and part of one 1/2 inch sheet ($24^1/_2$" x $79^1/_2$") for a medium size.

A power saw: A circular saw is adequate but a table saw will make cleaner, more accurate, cuts. The lumberyard can make the cuts for you, for a small fee.

A power drill

Wood screws: $1^1/_2$ inch

Wood glue

A jig saw: (optional) You will need this saw to form the curve in the legs.

Nails: (optional)

Handles: (optional but very convenient) You can find handles at the hardware store. Handles on the ends are useful in narrow hallways.

Instructions: If the saw cuts are made cleanly the box can be strong and tight.

1. Decide which size you will be making and cut the plywood accordingly.

   Cut the ends of the casket to the same height as the sides unless you are extending the length of the ends to form legs.

   Mark the curved shape of the legs with a round template and cut with the jig saw.

   If you like, you can cut and glue side leg facing from the curved scrap you cut from the ends.

·Simple Homemade Casket

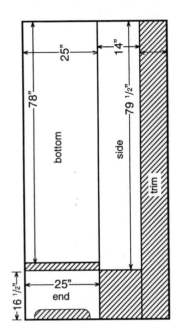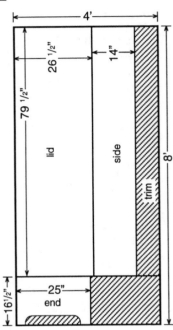

large

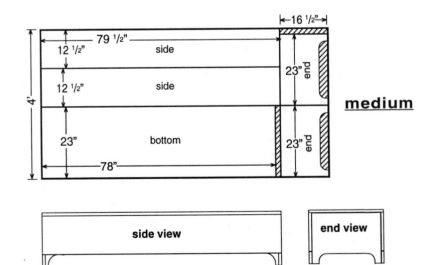

medium

side view

end view

2. Pre-drill the screw holes about eight inches apart on the sides, two to three inches apart on the ends.

If you have used extended end pieces for legs, mark a line on the end piece at the height of the side so that you know where to drill the holes.

3. Apply a thin bead of glue to the edge of the base.

If you are going to disassemble the casket, for reassembly later on, omit this step.

4. Glue and screw the end pieces to the base.

If the casket has legs, pile books under the base until the base lines up with the holes in the ends to make it easier to insert the screws.

5. Glue and screw the sides of the box.

You can give the casket a finished look by:

- applying a stain or varnish.

- adding a cloth liner.

- making a bier or a stand for the casket to rest on during the ceremony.

- covering the casket with a flag or cloth pall.

- covering the casket with photos or drawings.

TRANSPORTATION

The back of a station wagon, van, or pick-up truck is good transportation. Make sure that the casket is secure inside so that it won't move around. If a friend with a suitable vehicle can't be found, you can rent a van for a few hours or even hire a taxi.

An alternative is to hire a mortuary transportation service. These services, listed under "Funeral Director Supplies and Services" in the yellow pages of the telephone book, exist as a result of funeral home outsourcing. They are independent drivers, used by a number of funeral homes in an area to avoid the cost of in-house limousines and personnel. A funeral transportation service may not advertise but may, in fact, be available for hire.

While the family may hire someone without a special license to help with transportation, only a licensed funeral director can be hired to file the death certificate and obtain the disposition-transit permit from the Department of Health.

CEREMONY

There are different names for the ceremonies associated with a death. The gathering immediately after the death with the body present is called a *funeral ceremony*. During a funeral ceremony friends and family come together to accompany the body on its final journey to the cemetery or the crematory. There may be a formal "viewing" of the body at this time. There may be a collection taken so guests can help to defray funeral expenses or contribute to a memorial fund.

The gathering at the gravesite is called a *commitment ceremony*. It is usually a short simple ceremony to mark the lowering of the body into the grave.

Any gathering held after the burial or cremation is complete is a *memorial ceremony*. The memorial ceremony is held at any time and at any place, even months after the death, in a city far from where it occurred.

If you are planning a formal funeral or commitment service, select the person who will preside as early as possible. Decide on a time and place for the gathering so that friends can be told in plenty of time. There are many possible places to hold a service – a church, a temple, a public hall, in someone's home, even under a tree.

The formalities can be extremely simple, with just a few words to describe how you are marking this occasion. You may decide to ask a clergyman to perform a traditional funeral ceremony. Or, you may decide to have those who gather for the occasion express the fullness of the moment with their own words, rituals, music, and prayers. The ceremony can have the spirit of prayer or of celebration.

Some families have no formal ceremony at all. Even then, in the simplest situation, as family and friends wait with the body until the paperwork is complete, and then carry it to the cemetery or crematory, their activities become, naturally, and without calculation, a dignified ceremony. All of life has a special quality in the light of death.

The formal funeral service usually focuses on the positive qualities of the one who has died, and then, on the needs of the survivors. What can we learn? What is the legacy? What have we lost? In what spirit do we continue? We express both our loving attachment and our willingness to let go and accept what is. In the West the funeral is for the survivors.

Outside of Western culture the focus of the funeral ceremony may not be so much on the surviving family but on the continued journey of the deceased in the transition without the body. In this case, family and friends are gathered in encouragement and in prayer for the well-being of the departed soul during the next phase of being. Their focus is on the deceased. Personal grief, per se, is sometimes put aside at this time.

THE LEGAL REQUIREMENTS

WHO CAN TAKE RESPONSIBILITY

Family, Friends, and Religious Groups

Funeral Director Required

HOW IT WORKS

PAPERWORK

The Death Certificate

The Disposition - Transit Permit

The Cremation Permit

TIMING FOR THE PAPERWORK

THE MEDICAL EXAMINER

Autopsy

Contagious Diseases

 THE LEGAL REQUIREMENTS

WHO CAN TAKE RESPONSIBILITY

Family, Friends and Religious Groups

In most states, providing the funeral is not only the family's legal responsibility, it is their right. The family does not have to relinquish this right to a commercial funeral director unless there is some danger to the public health or safety. A number of states, however, have taken from the family the right of providing the funeral. Connecticut, Illinois, Indiana, Louisiana, Michigan, Nebraska, New Hampshire, New Jersey, and New York insist that a commercial funeral director be hired for every death. The financial responsibility in these states remains with the family.

The responsibility to provide and pay for the funeral falls to the next of kin within the family. The hierarchy for determining the next of kin is:

1. The surviving spouse

2. *All* the adult children

3. Both parents

4. *All* the siblings

Notice that when there is no surviving spouse, *all* of the adult children of the deceased must agree on a course of action for it to be carried out. For example, when cremation is considered, if all the adult children are not available to approve the cremation, the facility may insist that the body be buried. This may cost the family considerably more.

In most of the states in which non-commercial funerals are permitted, as long as there are no objections from the family, the funeral arrangements can be made by a friend or an unmarried partner.

When the family does object to a friend or an unmarried partner making the funeral arrangements, the friend or unmarried partner must have specific written authority from the dying person in order to proceed. The authorizing document needed is either a durable power of attorney or a valid will. This document must be in the hands of the friend who will need it immediately after the death, not in a safety deposit box which might not be opened for weeks.

States vary in their requirements for a valid durable power of attorney or will. In some states a simple signature is sufficient, but in others it must be notarized and signed by two witnesses. Giving someone a power of attorney for health care will not be adequate for making the funeral arrangements since this power becomes void upon death.

Maine, Wisconsin, and Wyoming will issue a disposition-transit permit only to those with a legal relationship to the deceased. In all cases friends and unmarried partners in these states must obtain written authorization, either from the dying person or from the next of kin, to make the funeral arrangements.

Four states - Colorado, Minnesota, Ohio, and West Virginia - give specific recognition to the rights of religious groups to make the funeral arrangements for their own community members.

A chart of state funeral regulations is in the appendix.

Funeral Director Required

In eight or nine states a licensed funeral director must be involved, to one degree or another, in every death.

In Illinois and Indiana the family can provide private transportation, but a funeral director must obtain the disposition-transit permit.

Six states, Louisiana, Michigan, Nebraska, New Hampshire, New Jersey, and New York prohibit all aspects of the family funeral. Even in some of these states, however, it is not unheard of for families, that are clear in their intent and willing to follow all Department of Health regulations, to convince officials to allow them to make the funeral arrangements without professional intervention. Department of Health regulations in Connecticut are confusing. Some statutes seem to permit family funerals; others do not.

HOW IT WORKS

State Departments of Health make sure that each funeral takes place in a dignified, timely, and legal manner. Although non-commercial funerals may be permitted in your state, they may be unusual. You may come across a clerk who is hesitant and needs to check further before proceeding. When officials realize that the family intends to follow all the regulations rather than to avoid them, they will usually be helpful and cooperative.

Home health agencies, hospitals, physicians, crematories, and cemeteries are used to cooperating with professional funeral directors, not with families. They may not fully understand your intentions at first. If they have questions about the non-commercial funeral, you can refer them to the registrar of Vital Statistics at the Department of Health. Once they understand what you are doing, you can work together to anticipate practical difficulties that may arise.

In particular, since it will be your responsibility to obtain the signed death certificate immediately after the death, remind the physician to have a blank form available to sign. Then, if the signed form is left at the hospital, make sure the hospital staff will release it to you when you arrive. If you think through these potential obstacles with the people involved the funeral should proceed without bureaucratic delay.

Home Death - Anticipated

Immediately after the death, call the physician or the home health agency. If 911 is called the emergency unit will have to take the body to the hospital to determine the cause of death. Although the family can reclaim the body at the hospital later, this inconvenience can be avoided by not calling 911 when the dying person has been under a physician's immediate care at home.

When death occurs in a private home, the police are summoned so that they can report that the death resulted from natural causes and that there was no foul play. In some communities the police have an agreement with home health agencies that enables them to write their report without coming to the house when death has been anticipated.

Home Death - Unexpected

When an unexpected death occurs at home, call your physician or 911 (examples are heart attacks, suicide and accidents). The body will be taken to the hospital so that a physician can determine the cause of death.

An autopsy maybe required when the cause of death is unclear. Once the autopsy and the death certificate are complete, and the disposition-transit permit is in hand, the hospital can release the body to you so that you can proceed with the funeral.

Hospital or Nursing Home Death

It is a good idea to have a plan worked out in advance with the facility so that they know that you will be serving as your own funeral director. Ask what they require in order to release the body and the death certificate to you after the death. To further insure that there are no mistakes, ask the staff to include these arrangements in the patient's "plan of care".

It is helpful when the facility can provide you with a private room to prepare the body for the funeral and to say good-bye. Time may be an issue for the hospital or nursing home. If you need more time to complete the paperwork than the hospital or nursing home will allow you, you can bring the body home in the casket or inquire whether they can keep the body at their morgue until preparations are complete.

PAPERWORK

The Death Certificate
The Disposition - Transit Permit
The Cremation Permit

Two forms are required for every death, the death certificate and the burial or disposition-transit permit. The death certificate is an official description of the person who died and the circumstances of the death. The disposition-transit permit enables the government to monitor public health and safety by tracking where the body is buried or cremated.

A third form is sometimes required when the Medical Examiner is called in to reconfirm the cause of death prior to cremation.

The Death Certificate

The death certificate is an important document. It must be filled out with complete accuracy. The information on it is used by the government to monitor public health, to make health policy, and to conduct medical research. The family will use certified copies of the death certificate to claim Social Security and other insurance benefits, to clear vehicle and property titles, and to settle financial obligations.

The death certificate is divided into two sections, the medical section and the family history section. The medical section, to be filled out and signed by the certifying physician within a day or two of death, contains information about the cause and the time of death. The physician states the cause of death in "wording that follows national guidelines". Someone in the family should look over this part of the certificate when it is received from the physician to make sure that it makes sense, that there are no blank spaces, that it is signed on the correct line, in black ink, and dated correctly. Inadvertent mistakes on the death certificate can cause frustrating delays.

The person who knows most about family names, dates, and spelling should provide the information for the part of the death certificate dealing with family history. The particular information asked for can be found in the "Death Certificate" section of the appendix.

A fetal death that occurs after twenty weeks of gestation, or after the fetus has attained 350 grams, must be reported by a physician to the Department of Health. In Georgia, Oregon, Nevada, Utah, and Virginia all fetal deaths, no matter how early in the pregnancy, must be reported to the Department of Health. See the "Chart of State Funeral Regulations" in the appendix for more specifics.

When you file the signed death certificate with the Department of Health, it's a good idea to ask for a dozen or more certified copies for later use. They will cost a few dollars each. These original certified copies of the death certificate will be required for settling the affairs of the deceased.

The Disposition-Transit Permit

The death certificate must be filled out properly and signed by the physician before the Department of Health will issue the disposition-transit permit. Do not transport the body without obtaining this permission. The cemetery or crematory will expect you to give the permit to them when you arrive. Check with them to make sure that they will file this permit with the Department of Health when disposition is complete.

When the burial takes place in a private rural cemetery, with no official in charge, it will be up to you to return the disposition-transit permit to the Department of Health. Make note on the returned permit that no official was in charge of the cemetery.

If the death occurs on a weekend and the Department of Health has no one "on call" to issue a disposition-transit permit, you can either wait until the office opens to file the death certificate and obtain the permit, or you can contact a local funeral director, or the Medical Examiner, who will probably be able to issue one. When a funeral director is thus acting as a registrar for the state, there should be no fee.

Again, if there is a long delay after the death, the body may need refrigeration.

The Cremation Permit

Cremation is a final and irreversible process. For this reason a number of states insist that the county Medical Examiner examine the body prior to cremation in order to make absolutely certain that the death occurred from natural causes. If needed, the crematory can arrange for the examination at their facility. A list of the states which require a cremation permit can be found in the "Chart of State Funeral Regulations" in the appendix.

The permission to cremate signed by the Medical Examiner in certain states should be distinguished from another permission form which the crematory will require the family to sign. On this second form, the next of kin permits the crematory to perform the cremation. Its purpose is to protect the facility from relatives who might appear later, claiming that they were not consulted before the cremation.

TIMING FOR THE PAPERWORK

Details vary from place to place but each state has a schedule for the completion of the funeral paperwork. In general, the physician must sign the death certificate within 24 or 48 hours of the death. The signed certificate is to be presented to the Department of Health a day or so after that. The disposition-transit permit, issued by the Department of Health must be returned to them by those in charge of the cemetery or crematory a week or so later.

The timing for the paperwork in each state is detailed in the "Chart of State Funeral Regulations" in the appendix. When families act as their own funeral directors they should have no trouble with timing because all of their paperwork will be completed prior to burial or cremation and so, well within any guidelines set.

THE MEDICAL EXAMINER
Autopsy
Contagious Diseases

Autopsy

When the cause of death is unclear an autopsy will need to be performed. This is often the job of the Medical Examiner. Sometimes the family requests an autopsy when the cause of death affects insurance settlements, but usually the autopsy is requested by the physician for public health reasons and there is no charge. In either case, when a family funeral is planned, tell the physician ahead of time so that the body will be clean and closed properly when the examination is complete.

Contagious Diseases

There are certain highly contagious diseases that require notification of the county Medical Examiner before a funeral can take place. The kinds of diseases usually requiring this notification are: plague, Asiatic cholera, small pox, and typhus fever. Only a few states consider AIDS, hepatitis, and tuberculosis highly contagious in this context.

When the presence of one of these contagious diseases is reported to the Department of Health, the Medical Examiner will be called and a professional funeral director may be required.

BURIAL OR CREMATION

FINDING A CEMETERY OR CREMATORY

BURIAL

Choices at the Cemetery
Paying for the Burial

CREMATION

BODY AND ORGAN DONATION

 BURIAL OR CREMATION

Throughout the ages, peoples of the earth have made use of the traditional four elements of earth, air, fire and water to dispose of their dead. Some of them have allowed their dead to decompose in the open air, some have practiced water burial. In the United States our choice, for the most part, is limited to earth or fire; burial or cremation.

Making this final decision between burial and cremation is a personal one. It is best considered and talked about before death occurs, because there are different perspectives. For some, having a "final resting place" in the countryside or in a plot near one's family is ideal. For some, cremation is seen as the traditional choice, or the only practical, economic choice in today's urban United States.

Legally speaking, burial is the presumed choice. Cremation must be specifically elected if it is desired.

The wishes of the next of kin are usually honored with regard to disposition of the body. A few states, Texas and Washington among them, will allow you to sign a "permit to cremate" form before your own death, but usually, the next of kin decides. So those who have strong feelings about their own burial or cremation should let their family know their wishes.

FINDING THE CEMETERY OR CREMATORY

It is best if you can select the cemetery you will use before the death occurs. Remember, the corporate cemetery is in the business of selling real estate. If you wait until the day the decision must be made, you are at a bargaining disadvantage. Your choices will be greatly improved if you find out ahead of time what is available in your community.

One way to find out about your local resources is to join a chapter of the non-profit Funeral and Memorial Society. Their address is in the white pages of your telephone book.

On your initial contact with the cemetery or crematory, tell them that the family will be serving as the funeral director. Let them know that you understand the responsibilities, that you will file the death certificate, provide transportation and present them with the disposition-transit permit when you arrive.

Increasingly, in the United States, the cemetery and crematory are owned by the same corporation that owns the funeral home. This does not mean that the cemetery will be unwilling to accommodate a family funeral, but don't be too surprised if they offer some discouraging words. They may try to convince you that this is an overwhelming task bureaucratically and emotionally or that the very idea of a non-commercial funeral is somehow strange. Understand what their interests are and use your own judgment.

If it is difficult to find a crematory or cemetery that will work with you, you might want to contact your state consumer protection agency to inform them of your difficulty.

Not all cemeteries are businesses. There are non-profit cemeteries run by religious groups, municipalities and the federal government. Veterans may be entitled to burial in a veterans' cemetery but not necessarily near their home.

There are those in the United States and the United Kingdom who seek to combine community cemeteries with natural wildlife reserves. Grave sites could be marked by a tree, a bench or a small plaque. See the Natural Death Centre in the "Where to Get More Help" section of the appendix.

A body can be buried or cremated only in a place which is permitted for that purpose by the county. You cannot bury a body in your back yard or "the back forty" without permission from the county zoning department. Before you decide to dedicate part of your land as a cemetery, understand that it may make the property more difficult to sell in the future and, once sold, it may be difficult for the family to visit the grave site.

BURIAL

Choices at the Cemetery

You choose a particular cemetery because it is nearby, well cared for, beautiful, within the budget, or because you already own a plot there.

Each cemetery has its own standards and regulations. Some will allow you to plant a tree over the grave or have other individual expressions. Others will insist that memorials be of a standard size and style. Some will make it easy for the family that wants to help dig and refill the grave; others will not. Most will insist that you purchase an outer container, a grave liner or a reinforced concrete vault, to limit the settlement of soil over time. By law, all will permit the use of homemade caskets without the imposition of any extra charges.

The cost of the burial varies from no cost at all to thousands of dollars. There are cemeteries in rural areas that offer free space. You do the digging or pay someone for the service. In these cemeteries, care of the grave site over the years will be up to the family. A cemetery plot in a "desirable" urban location, with perpetual care of the grounds can cost thousands of dollars.

When you are deciding between different cemeteries, compare the quality and cost of the following:

Grave Site: The cost to purchase a grave site or cemetery plot. You can expect to pay from a few hundred dollars to many thousands of dollars for a choice site with a view.

Preparation of the Grave Site: The cost of digging and filling the grave. Few large cemeteries will allow anyone but their own staff to dig and fill the grave but, if this is important to you, there is no harm in asking. Be forewarned, digging the grave by hand is a difficult, all day, affair. Local regulations will stipulate how deep the top of the casket must be below the level of the surrounding soil.

In order to lower heavy commercial caskets into the grave, cemeteries use a large mechanical device. If you desire, you can lower a lighter-weight wood or corrugated cardboard casket into the earth with hand held ropes or straps.

Grave Liner or Vault: The cost to purchase a concrete grave liner or vault. A liner is thinner concrete, and costs a few hundred dollars. A vault is reinforced concrete and more expensive. Purchase of a liner or vault is not a legal or a health requirement. The cemetery usually insists on this purchase to save themselves from having to backfill when the soil settles in the grave over time.

Headstones and Markers: The cost and choice of headstones and markers. Many cemeteries restrict the use of upright headstones, plantings, or other memorials. They encourage markers that are uniform and flush to the ground, giving an orderly feel to the grounds and making cemetery maintenance easier. Some cemeteries insist that you purchase the memorial stone or marker from them, instead of from an outside supplier.

Care and Maintenance: The cost of perpetual care and maintenance of the common grounds and the individual grave. Ask what is included in these costs.

Record Keeping: The cost of record keeping.

Paying for the Burial

When it comes to buying the plot, the American Association of Retired Persons (AARP) and the editors of *Consumer Reports* magazine, warn against purchasing with the preneed, prepay plans marketed extensively by the funeral and the insurance industries.

While these citizen groups encourage people to *plan* their funeral and burial ahead of time, they discourage *paying* ahead of time with these preneed plans. They point out that although paying for the burial in advance may seem a good idea because it "locks in" today's prices, there are many ways for consumers to lose their investments.

If you are inclined to invest in a prepay burial plan in order to secure a particular burial site, or to "lock in" today's prices, understand the answers to the following questions before you invest.

- What happens if the cemetery goes bankrupt?
- What happens if they sell the business to someone who doesn't honor the agreement?
- What happens if the family moves to another area? Sometimes the contract can be transferred.
- What happens if the family changes its mind? Some cemeteries will buy the plot back, but at a price much less than what was paid by your family.
- What happens if you choose to purchase a memorial stone or other funeral goods from another company? Some contracts lock you into a single source for your purchases.
- What happens if the family cannot pay all at once? Sometimes the payments can be spread over time.
- What happens to accrued interest in the account?
- What happens to any funds remaining in the account after the funeral?

Notice also that some cemetery services, such as digging and filling the grave, are not part of the prepayment contract and must be paid for at the time of death.

If your purpose in buying the plan is to avoid inflationary price increases, make sure that you ask for a guaranteed price plan.

An alternative to signing a prepayment contract with a cemetery or insurance company is a "pay on death" savings account called a Totten Trust which is set up at a local bank. The trust account has a named beneficiary who is paid the proceeds of the account at the time of death and must use the funds according to specified instructions.

Until needed the Totten Trust will earn interest to offset inflation. It will enable you to move your home or change your mind and the fund can be redirected if a family emergency arises prior to the death.

CREMATION

To find your local crematory look up Cemeteries and Memorial Parks in the yellow pages of your telephone book.

In years past, cremating the body was an unceremonious and matter-of-fact event. But today the same options that are offered by the funeral industry for burial are offered for cremation, including preparing the body for family viewing and providing caskets for rent or purchase. Cremation alone, without added options, will probably cost between $100 and $500.

By law, no casket is required for cremation though the facility may require a minimum "cremation box" of corrugated cardboard for the safety of their staff. During the cremation process the body is placed in a retort. The retort is an oven which reaches extremely high temperatures. Within a few hours the body and the container it was brought in are reduced to a few pounds of ash and bone fragments. Before the cremated remains are returned to you, the bone fragments will be mechanically pulverized to reduce them to a more powdery consistency suitable for scattering.

You can give your own urn or container to the crematory staff when you arrive or they will provide you with a simple box. Your container should be at least 300 cubic inches (6 x 6 x 9 inches or gallon-size) for an adult. Be aware that a wooden casket produces more ash than a corrugated cardboard box.

Don't forget to remove any valuables that you want to keep before the cremation takes place.

Because a Pacemaker contains lithium, it can explode in the heat of the retort if it is not removed prior to cremation. The Pacemaker is a small disk located just under the skin on the chest that can be removed by the crematory staff, by the medical person who fills out the death certificate or by a family member.

Some families wait the few hours it takes to complete the cremation. There may be a room set aside for this purpose. If you decide not to wait, the cremated remains can be sent to your home by mail. It is often an emotional experience when they arrive so you might want to ask a friend over for the occasion.

Only a few states have restrictions on the disposition of cremated remains. Families have a range of choices including having them scattered on land or at sea, placed in a columbarium on the church or crematory grounds, buried at a cemetery, stored at home or placed in a shrine. In California, cremated remains may not be scattered or buried on public or private land without a specific permit from the Department of Health.

BODY AND ORGAN DONATION

Plans for donating a body to medical education must be made with the anatomy department of a local medical school before death takes place. Sometimes, even though prior arrangements had been made, the medical school declines the donation, so alternative plans may still be needed. Age and the cause of death are factors in their acceptance decision.

There can be a family funeral after an organ donation. Most organ donations originate when the medical staff from the intensive care unit of the hospital approaches the family to ask about the possibility. The family of someone relatively young and dying of an injury is most likely to be approached.

You can indicate your intention to become an organ donor on a Uniform Donor Card, available from the Red Cross or a local hospital. If you want to be a donor, it is very important to tell your family in advance because, Donor Card or not, the hospital will honor the wishes of the next of kin in this matter. The American Red Cross can arrange for donations of heart valves, bone, cornea, and other tissue. Call 1-800-284-7783, or call the National Kidney Foundation at 1-800-622-9010.

To receive a free brochure on becoming an organ or tissue donor call 1-888-55SHARE.

A P P E N D I X E S

FUNERAL PLANNING GUIDE

CHECKLIST FOR
THE DAY OF THE FUNERAL

THE DEATH CERTIFICATE

THE OBITUARY NOTICE

COMMERCIAL FUNERAL OPTIONS

CHART OF STATE FUNERAL
REGULATIONS

WHERE TO GET MORE HELP

LETTING GO SLOWLY (A POEM)

FUNERAL PLANNING GUIDE

BRING THE PAPERWORK TOGETHER

❑ Locate important family documents such as the will, safety deposit box numbers and keys, bank accounts, insurance policies, credit cards, body and organ donation documents, deed for a cemetery lot, and previously signed permission to cremate.

❑ Gather the information needed for the death certificate and the obituary.

❑ Gather the photos, music, and readings you will use for the ceremony.

❑ Obtain the blank book that will be used for recording the messages left by mourners.

NOTIFICATIONS OF THE DEATH

❑ Make a list of the names and phone numbers of those you will notify at the time of death: the physician or home health agency, the police, the Department of Health, immediate family, close friends, employer, colleagues, attorney, and the executor of the estate.

❑ Make a list of those you will notify soon after the death: the post office, newspaper delivery service, the landlord, and the utility companies.

HOSPITAL OR NURSING HOME DEATH

❑ Inform the staff of the facility of your intention to make the funeral arrangements yourselves.

❑ Determine their requirements for releasing the death certificate and the body to you.

❑ Determine whether the facility will be able to provide you with a private room for the preparation of the body and a ceremony.

DEPARTMENT OF HEALTH

❑ Locate the nearest office of the Department of Health. Tell them your plans, determine their office hours, and ask how you can obtain a deposition-transit permit if the death occurs on a weekend.

Address

Phone

Office hours

Weekend options

CEMETERY OR CREMATORY

❑ Decide which crematory or cemetery you will work with.

Name

Address

Phone

❑ What are their hours of operation.

CARE OF THE BODY

❑ Arrange for a casket or a pallet.

Who will provide it

Phone

❑ Gather soap, oils, brushes, towels, plastic sheeting, and clothing that will be used for the preparation of the body.

❑ Arrange for a transporting vehicle.

Who's vehicle

Phone

CEREMONY

❑ Decide whether you will have a funeral service, a commitment service, and/or a memorial service.

❑ Determine who will lead the service and make sure that they are available.

Name

Phone

❑ Decide where the ceremony will be held.

Name

Address

Phone

❑ Decide who the pall bearers will be.

❑ Decide where donations can be sent.

❑ Plan for any special memorials or epitaphs.

PETS

❑ Provide for the care of all the pets.

CHECKLIST FOR THE
DAY OF THE FUNERAL

WHEN DEATH FIRST OCCURS

❑ Take the time you need to become calm. Remember, this is not an emergency.

❑ When you are ready, gather those closest to express their good-byes and prayers.

❑ Call the physician, home health agency, or 911, whichever is appropriate, to tell them that the death has occurred.

❑ Make arrangements for the physician to provide you with the signed death certificate.

❑ Find the nearest office of the Department of Health. Inform them of your plans and determine their office hours.

❑ Notify the police if this has been a home death.

❑ Contact the cemetery or crematory you will be using and schedule an appointment.

❑ Arrange for a transporting vehicle.

❑ Arrange for the casket or pallet.

CARING FOR THE BODY

❑ If you are going to wash dress and lay out the body, do so within an hour or so of the death.

❑ Make arrangements for keeping the body cool, if necessary.

PAPERWORK

❑ Complete the family history section of the death certificate that you receive from the physician.

❑ File the signed death certificate with the Department of Health and obtain a disposition-transit permit from them.

❑ Get extra copies of the certified death certificate from the Department of Health.

❑ Locate ownership documents of a cemetery plot.

❑ Locate plans for the funeral ceremony.

CEREMONY

☐ Contact the person who will lead the funeral ceremony and confirm a time and place.

☐ Make sure that the gathering place is available and prepared.

☐ Inform friends and family of the ceremony arrangements.

☐ Collect the readings, music, prayers and meditations that will be part of the service.

☐ Gather for the formalities.

CEMETERY OR CREMATORY

☐ Reconfirm your arrival time with the cemetery or crematory before you leave.

☐ Transport the body to the cemetery or crematory.

☐ Give the disposition-transit permit to the staff when you arrive.

☐ Make sure that they will return the form to the Department of Health.

THE DEATH CERTIFICATE

The death certificate is used by the government to collect statistical data. It is important that there are no mistakes on the form and no unanswered questions.

The death certificate must:

- be typed (preferably) or printed and signed in black ink.
- have true, original signatures. No rubber stamps or copies are allowed.
- contain no erasures, "white-out", or cross outs.
- have no blank spaces. All questions must be answered but "unknown" can be an appropriate response.
- must contain no abbreviations other than for the names of the months. Numbers for months are not permitted.

The death certificate is divided into two sections. The information in the first section is provided by the family, specifically by someone called the "informant". The informant may or may not be the same person who is actually filling out the death certificate. The informant is the person most knowledgeable about family names, spelling, and dates.

QUESTIONS ABOUT THE DECEASED:

Full Name:

Date of Birth: *spell out name of month*

State or Country of Birth: *do not abbreviate*

Citizenship: *do not abbreviate*

Marital Status: *check "married" if separated but still legally married*

Surviving Spouse: *if wife, use maiden name*

Usual Occupation: *work done during most of life e.g. secretary, manager, student, housewife. "Retired" is not acceptable "retired secretary" is acceptable.*

Kind of Business or Industry: *e.g. government, education, manufacturing, "own home" is O.K. for housewife/househusband*

Race: White, Black, American Indian   *if group not specified write national origin*

Is Person of Spanish Origin   Y   N: *specify Cuban, Mexican, other*

Social Security Number:

Residence Address:

United States Armed Forces Y N: *specify branch*

Education*: highest grade completed*

QUESTIONS ABOUT OTHERS

Father's Full Name:

Mother's Full Name:

Informant's Full Name and Mailing Address:
in case the authorities have any further questions

QUESTIONS ABOUT THE PLACE AND TIME OF DEATH

Hospital or Institution Name: *if there is no institution, give the street name and the number of the house. If the death was from an accident, give the names of the cross streets.*

QUESTIONS ABOUT DISPOSITION

Method of Disposition: *Burial, Cremation, Entombment, or Donation*

Cemetery or Crematory:

Name:

Address:

Disposition-Transit Permit Number:

Funeral Director: *name of the person actually filling out the death certificate as distinct from the name of the "informant" who provides the information.*

Funeral Home Name: *the appropriate response, since there is no funeral home, is to give the relationship of the "funeral director" above, to the deceased, i.e. sister, nurse, hospice volunteer.*

License Number of Funeral Director: *write "none".*

The second section of the death certificate is to be filled out by the certifying physician. It is the physician's responsibility to state the cause of death in "wording that follows national guidelines". Someone in the family should look over this part of the certificate when it is received from the physician to make sure that it makes sense, that there are no blank spaces, that it is signed on the correct line, in black ink and dated correctly.

THE OBITUARY NOTICE

Local newspapers carry the obituaries of residents, and sometimes, of former residents, as a public service. Information about the deceased that they will accept for publication includes: name, age, occupation, place of residence, clubs, organizations and affiliations, military status, service times and locations, names of survivors, attire for those attending services, requests for donations, and whether or not flowers are desired.

Certain newspapers offer the opportunity for a more flexible and more personal expression than these dry details. They allow individuals, for a fee, to write their own obituary, perhaps a legacy to pass on to others. Call your local newspaper to see what can be arranged.

COMMERCIAL FUNERAL OPTIONS

The Federal Trade Commission oversees the professional business practices of the funeral industry by means of the Funeral Rule. Most of their efforts have gone to assuring that inexpensive options are made available to the consumer and that the prices for funeral goods and services are disclosed.

According to the Funeral Rule, funeral providers must give you pricing information over the telephone. If you inquire in person they must give you both a written General Price List that reveals your legal rights, and a written Casket Price List. They may not charge a "contagious disease" fee or a fee for "protective clothing". The General Price List starts off with a Minimum Professional Fee. This fee will be charged no matter which funeral arrangements you select.

When you hire a funeral director to be in charge of the funeral you are offered two basic styles of service, Direct Disposition and the Traditional American Funeral.

DIRECT DISPOSITION

In recent years Americans have shown increasing interest in direct cremation or immediate burial services. These minimum services offered by the funeral director or by a direct disposition company like the Neptune Society, are basically pickup and delivery services. With direct disposition the funeral provider files the death certificate with the Department of Health and transports the body from the place of death to the crematory or to the cemetery. Their facilities are not used. There is no viewing, no funeral ceremony, and no family participation. Charges range from $700-$1,600 or higher.

THE TRADITIONAL AMERICAN FUNERAL

The Traditional American Funeral is the standard of service in the funeral industry. This funeral centers on the practice of the family viewing the body in the funeral home days after the death has occurred. For this occasion the body is embalmed, dressed, cosmetized, coiffed, and casketed. The double door casket reveals the deceased as if asleep on a luxurious mattress and pillow. A ceremony at the church or the funeral home follows, and perhaps a commitment service at the grave site. This funeral costs about $5,000. Burial and memorial stones are additional.

CHART OF STATE FUNERAL REGULATIONS

Each state keeps track of who dies and makes sure that the funeral takes place in a safe and timely fashion. Most of the funeral regulations summarized in the following chart are part of the Vital Statistics section of the state Health Code. To confirm that you are in compliance with the most recent regulations call you local Department of Health.

Additional state statutes regulate the safety and ethical business practices of funeral homes, cemeteries, and crematories. These business regulations are monitored by State Funeral Boards and Departments of Commerce and Consumer Affairs. We will not discuss them here.

Funeral regulations cover the following areas of concern:

Permitting Legislation: The state statute or rule which specifies who can be legally responsible for the funeral.

In Charge: Who, according to the statute, can be responsible for the funeral: any "person", a "family" member only, or a "funeral director".

Time Schedule: Disposition must be completed, or the body refrigerated within this limit. In most states no specific time is given. Weather is a consideration. Good judgment is required.

File Within: The completed, signed death certificate must be filed with the Department of Health within the stated number of days of the death.

Cremation Permit: In certain states a cremation permit must be issued and signed by the Medical Examiner before cremation can take place.

Cremation Wait: The waiting period required before cremation can take place.

STATE FUNERAL REGULATIONS

Permitting Legislation	In Charge	Time Schedule	Sign Within	File Within	Cremation Permit	Waiting Period	Comments
ALABAMA Vit Stat. 22-9-14	person	reasonable	5 days	5 days	need	no	
ALASKA AC Title 7 05.410	person	reasonable	24 hours	3 days	need	no	
ARIZONA AC 9-19-326	person	24 hours	3 days	3 days	need	no	Time from issue of transit permit to disposition not to exceed 36 hours.
ARKANSAS VSA 20-18-601(b)	person	24 hrs for burial, 48 hrs for cremation	48 hours	10 days	need	no	Those infected with a communicable disease must be tagged.
CALIFORNIA H S 9.1.10.201	person	reasonable	15 hours	8 days	don't need	no	A permit is needed to scatter cremated remains
COLORADO Title 25 Article 2-110	person	24 hours	48 hours	5 days	don't need	no	

STATE FUNERAL REGULATIONS

Permitting Legislation	In Charge	Time Schedule	Sign Within	File Within	Cremation Permit	Waiting Period	Comments
CONNECTICUT	uncertain	reasonable	24 hours	—	need	48 hours	Laws seem to conflict. Consult the Health Dept.
DELAWARE Code 31.16.3123(b)	person	reasonable	48 hours	3 days	need	no	
DISTRICT OF COLUMBIA Title 6-211	person	reasonable	48 hours	5 days	need	no	
FLORIDA VSA 382.002(9)	person	24 hours	5 days	5 days	need	48 hours	
GEORGIA Code 31.10.15b	person	reasonable	72 hours	72 hours	need	no	Report all fetal deaths
HAWAII HR 338-1(5)	person	30 hours	24 hours	3 days	don't need	no	

STATE FUNERAL REGULATIONS

Permitting Legislation	In Charge	Time Schedule	Sign Within	File Within	Cremation Permit	Waiting Period	Comments
IDAHO Code 39.260 39.268	person	reasonable	72 hours	5 days	need	no	Notify the Health Department within 24 hours of the death.
ILLINOIS	funeral director	—	—	—	—	—	A funeral director must obtain the transit permit.
INDIANA	funeral director	—	—	—	—	—	A funeral director must obtain the transit permit.
IOWA Code 144.27	person	48 hours	24 hours	3 days	don't need	no	
KANSAS VSA 65.2 24.65	person	24 hours	3 days	3 days	need	no	
KENTUCKY RS 213.076	person	reasonable	5 days	5 days	need	no	

STATE FUNERAL REGULATIONS

Permitting Legislation	In Charge	Time Schedule	Sign Within	File Within	Cremation Permit	Waiting Period	Comments
MINNESOTA DHR 4610.08	person	72 hours	5 days	5 days	need	no	Transportation completed in 18 hours in a closed vehicle.
MISSISSIPPI H.D. 41.36.3 Rule 38	person	48 hours	72 hours	5 days	don't need	no	Transportation completed within 24 hours of death.
MISSOURI PHR 193.145.4	person	reasonable	72 hours	5 days	need	no	An identification tag must accompany the body.
MONTANA PH and SS 9.16.6.901(3)	person	reasonable	10 days	10 days	need	no	
NEBRASKA	funeral director	—	—	—	—	—	
NEVADA RS 440.450	person	reasonable	48 hours	72 hours	don't need	no	Report all fetal deaths.

STATE FUNERAL REGULATIONS

Permitting Legislation	In Charge	Time Schedule	Sign Within	File Within	Cremation Permit	Waiting Period	Comments
LOUISIANA RS 40.49A+50	uncertain	reasonable	24 hours	5 days	need	no	In practice, transit permits are issued only to licensed funeral directors.
MAINE Title 22.2842.1	family	reasonable	5 days	5 days	need	48 hours	If no one in the family is able to, anyone "authorized in writing" may take responsibility.
MARYLAND AHC Title 4-2	person	reasonable	24 hours	72 hours	don't need	12 hours	
MASSACHUSETTS MGL c114 s.45	person	reasonable	36 hours	36 hours	need	48 hours	Local departments of health decide whether to permit family funerals.
MICHIGAN	funeral director	—	—	—	—	—	

STATE FUNERAL REGULATIONS

Permitting Legislation	In Charge	Time Schedule	Sign Within	File Within	Cremation Permit	Waiting Period	Comments
NEW HAMPSHIRE	funeral director	—	—	—	—	—	
NEW JERSEY	funeral director	—	—	—	—	—	
NEW MEXICO VS 24.14.20 B and 2414-23	person	reasonable	2 days	5 days	need	no	
NEW YORK	funeral director	—	—	—	—	—	
NORTH CAROLINA VS 130A.113(b)	person	reasonable	3 days	5 days	need	no	
NORTH DAKOTA H S A 23.02.1-19.2	person	reasonable	8 days	15 days	need	no	
OHIO RC 3705.16	person	reasonable	48 hours	10 days	don't need	no	

STATE FUNERAL REGULATIONS

Permitting Legislation	In Charge	Time Schedule	Sign Within	File Within	Cremation Permit	Waiting Period	Comments
OKLAHOMA Title 59 Sec.3962 Title 63 1-317	person	reasonable	48 hours	3 days	need	no	
OREGON Chapter 432.307(2)	person	reasonable	48 hours	5 days	don't need	no	Notify Health Dept. within 24 hrs. Rpt. all fetal deaths.
PENNSYLVANIA Title 450.501	person	reasonable	96 hours	96 hours	don't need	24 hours	
RHODE ISLAND Title 23-3-18	person	reasonable	immediately	7 days	need	24 hours	
SOUTH CAROLINA Reg. 61.19.18(b)	person	reasonable	48 hours	5 days	need	24 hours	
SOUTH DAKOTA P.H.S. 34.25.25	person	reasonable	24 hours	10 days	need	24 hours	Notify Health Dept. before scattering ashes.
TENNESSEE Title 68.3.502:(3b)	person	reasonable	48 hours	5 days	need	no	

STATE FUNERAL REGULATIONS

Permitting Legislation	In Charge	Time Schedule	Sign Within	File Within	Cremation Permit	Waiting Period	Comments
TEXAS AC 25.181.2	person	reasonable	24 hours	10 days	don't need	48 hours	
UTAH Statutes 26.2.13.(4)	person	24 hours	72 hours	5 days	don't need	no	Report all fetal deaths.
VERMONT 18.5201.	person	24 hours	24 hours	—	need	no	
VIRGINIA Title 32.1-263.B	person	reasonable	24 hours	3 days	need	24 hours	Report all fetal deaths.
WASHINGTON RCW 70.58.170.240	person	24 hours	3 days	3 days	don't need	no	
WEST VIRGINIA 16.5.21	person	reasonable	24 hours	3 days	need	no	
WISCONSIN HSS 135.03	family	reasonable	5 days	9 days	need	48 hours	
WYOMING Title 35-1-5-2(a)	family	reasonable	24 hours	3 days	don't need	24 hours	

WHERE TO GET MORE HELP

ORGANIZATIONS

The American Association of Retired Persons (AARP) is a non-profit organization dedicated to helping older Americans achieve lives of independence, dignity, and purpose. They publish two free publications: *Funeral Goods and Services* and *Prepaying Your Funeral?*
601 E Street N.W., Washington, D.C. 20049
(202) 434-2214

The Compassionate Friends is a self-help support organization for those grieving for a child.
P.O. Box 3696 Oak Brook, IL 60522-3696
(630) 990-0010

Funeral and Memorial Societies of America is a cooperative, non-profit, consumer-advocacy organization which arranges with local mortuaries for discounted services and helps its members plan their funerals. Find your local group in the white pages of the telephone book.
FAMSA, P.O. Box 10, Hinesburg, VT 05461
www.funerals.org/famsa

The Living/Dying Project provides educational and support services for caregivers and those who know they are dying. They teach the possibility of personal transformation, spiritual awakening, and conscious dying.
Box 357 Fairfax, CA 94978 (415) 456-3915

National Hospice Organization helps families provide support for dying at home. Find your local Hospice in the White Pages. 1901 North Moore St., Suite 901, Arlington, VA 22209 (703) 243-5900

Natural Death Centre, USA dedicated to improving the quality of death: death midwives, non-commercial funeral, green burials.
P.O. Box 1721, Sebastopol, CA 95473
www.newciv.org/GIB   rhino@dial.pipex.com

Project on Death in America was organized by businessman/philanthropist George Soros. It focuses the medical, educational, and government agencies on dying and bereavement in order to help transform the culture and experience surrounding death in America.
mcallaway@sorosny.org   www.soros.org/death.html

Upaya: The Project on Being With Dying is a training program for professionals who want to incorporate contemplative perspectives with dying.
1404 Cerro Gordo Road, Santa Fe, NM 87501
(505)986-8518   www.rt.66.com/~upaya

Zen Hospice Project provides education, outreach, hospice services and trains volunteers who seek to cultivate wisdom and compassion through service. They offer consulting services for developing hospice programs. 273 Page Street, San Francisco, CA 94102
(415) 863-2910   www.zenhospice.org

BOOKS

The Art of Dying: How to Leave This World with Dignity and Grace, at Peace with Yourself and Your Loved Ones by Patricia Weenolsen

Being Peace by Thich Nhat Hanh

Being with Dying (audio tapes) by Joan Halifax

Coming Home: A Guide to Home Care for the Terminally Ill by Deborah Duda

Companion Through the Darkness: Inner Dialogues on Grief by Stephanie Ericsson

The Courage to Grieve by Judy Tatelbaum

Dealing Creatively With Death: A Manual of Death Education and Simple Burial by Ernest Morgan

Denial of the Soul: Spiritual and Medical Perspectives on Euthanasia and Mortality by M. Scott Peck

Dying Well: The Prospect for Growth at the End of Life by Dr. Ira Byock

Facing Death and Finding Hope: A Guide to the Physical and Emotional Care of the Dying by Christine Longaker

The Final Act of Love: Caring for Your Own Dead by Lisa Carlson

Final Acts of Love: Families, Friends, and Assisted Dying by Stephen Jamison, Ph.D.

Fire in the Soul: A New Psychology of Spiritual Optimism by Joan Borysenko, Ph.D.

A Good Death: Taking More Control at the End of Your Life for The National Council for the Right to Die by T. Patrick Hill and David Shirley

ORDER FORM

Please send _____copies of *Coming to Rest* to:

Name _____

Street or P.O. Box _____

City _____

State _____ Zip _____

I have enclosed: ❏ Money order ❏ Check

Charge my: ❏ Visa ❏ Mastercard

Name on card _____

Card billing address _____

City _____

State _____ Zip _____

Card No. _____

Expiration date _____

Signature _____

<u>Credit Card Orders</u> (800)431-1579
<u>Fax Orders</u> (914)835-0398
<u>Mail Orders:</u> Dovetail
              P.O. Box 1720
              Kamuela, HI 96743

First class postage paid for copies sent to the same address:
single copy $14.00
two copies $19.20
eight copies $57.60
Add two dollars for each additional address.
Please add 4% tax for orders sent to addresses in Hawaii

Julie Wiskind was educated at the University of Wisconsin and at Barnard College. The mother of three sons—Joey, Adam, and Gabriel—she has made her home in New York, Cleveland and Oakland and now on the Big Island of Hawaii. When she was eleven years old, Julie was sent away to the country for a few weeks to protect her from the trauma of her mother's death. She returned home only "after it was all over". This unceremonious and abrupt encounter with death changed Julie's life. Ever since, she has tried to remain present when death was near and to show up for life too, whenever possible. Julie is president of Dovetail, Resources for a Family Funeral. She is a hospice volunteer.

In 1970 Richard Spiegel left his small, "storefront" law practice in Washington, D.C. He arrived on the Big Island of Hawaii in 1974 where he became a beekeeper, started a community mediation center and, with Laura, raised their two daughters, Kristin and Shaina. After Laura died in 1993, Richard left his position as executive director of West Hawaii Mediation Services to get his feet back on the ground. He is now a full time beekeeper and owner of a small family apiary that supplies gourmet stores in Hawaii, California, New York and London with Rare Hawaiian White Honey.

ORDER FORM

Please send _____copies of *Coming to Rest* to:

Name _____

Street or P.O. Box _____

City _____

State _____ Zip _____

I have enclosed: ❏ Money order ❏ Check

Charge my: ❏ Visa ❏ Mastercard

Name on card _____

Card billing address _____

City _____

State _____ Zip _____

Card No. _____

Expiration date _____

Signature _____

<u>Credit Card Orders</u> (800)431-1579
<u>Fax Orders</u> (914)835-0398
<u>Mail Orders:</u> Dovetail
P.O. Box 1720
Kamuela, HI 96743

First class postage paid for copies sent to the same address:
single copy $14.00
two copies $19.20
eight copies $57.60
Add two dollars for each additional address.
Please add 4% tax for orders sent to addresses in Hawaii

May all beings be happy.

LETTING GO, SLOWLY

Richard Spiegel

slowly, slowly
you unravel from my life
string by string is loosed
as time moves on,
steady, unswerving
without you

sixteen years of sunsets
whether or not we took notice

and now
what remains
a constant flowing stream
of you
in me
memories, feelings
longings
moments long unthought resurface
bringing tears
sometimes, a quiet smile
now dusted with sadness

string by string
they appear
unraveling your presence

unweaving the blanket of our time
reweaving the circuits of my mind

The Good Death: The New American Search to Reshape the End of Life   by Marilyn Webb

The Grieving Child: A Parent's Guide
by Helen Fitzgerald

Healing into Life and Death   by Stephen Levine

How We Die: Reflections on Life's Final Chapter
by Sherwin Nuland

The Joy of Living and Dying in Peace
by H.H. the Dalai Lama

Learning to Say Goodbye: When a Parent Dies
by Eda Le Shan

Love, Medicine and Miracles
by Bernie S. Siegel, M.D.

Peace, Love and Healing
by Bernie S. Siegel, M.D.

Ready to Live Prepared to Die   by Amy Harwell

Signs of Life: A Memoir of Dying and Discovery
by Tim Brooks

Stay Close and Do Nothing: A Spiritual and Practical Guide to Caring for the Dying at Home
by Merrill Collett

The Tibetan Book of Living and Dying
by Sogyal Rinpoche

Who Dies?: An Investigation of Conscious Living and Conscious Dying   by Stephen Levine

Widow   by Lynn Caine

A Year to Live: How to Live This Year As If It Were Your Last   by Stephen Levine